09/05   18.96

BUILDING
WORLD LANDMARKS

The
Royal Gorge
Bridge

by Margaret Speaker Yuan

BLACKBIRCH®
PRESS

THOMSON
™
GALE

San Diego • Detroit • New York • San Francisco • Cleveland • New Haven, Conn. • Waterville, Maine • London • Munich

Photo credits: cover, pp. 36-37 © Joseph Sohm; ChromoSohm Inc./Corbis; pp. 8, 42 © Vince Streano/Corbis; pg. 10 © Erich Lessing/Art Resource, NY; pp. 7, 21 © Corel; pg. 18 © Mary Evans Picture Library; pg 22 © Carol Havens/Corbis; pg. 32 © Jm Wark/Lonely Planet; pp. 26, 34, 40, 43 © Royal Gorge Bridge & Park/Harris Photography; pp. 5 (GB-5952), 13 (GB-8341), 16 (GB-6023), 23 (GB-6003), 29 (GB-6012), 31 (GB-6011) © Denver Public Library, Western History Collection, George Beam; pp. 11 (X-17964), 17 (X-6971) © Denver Public Library, Western History Collection; pg. 14 (MCC-515) © Denver Public Library, Western History Collection, L. C. McClure; pg. 4 © Blackbirch Archive;

The author wishes to thank Mike Bandera and Denise Lallamande of the Royal Gorge Bridge and Park, and Susan K. Cochran of the Local History Center at the Cañon City Public Library for their help in providing archival materials used in the preparation of this book. Special thanks are due to Harold Witcher for answering the author's questions about his father.

LIBRARY OF CONGRESS CATALOGING-IN-PUBLICATION DATA

Yuan, Margaret Speaker
  Royal Gorge Bridge / By Margaret Speaker Yuan.
     p. cm. — (Building world landmarks)
Summary: Describes the techniques used and difficulties faced in building Colorado's Royal Gorge Bridge, the highest suspension bridge in the world and a popular tourist attraction.
Includes bibliographical references and index.
  ISBN 1-56711-352-4 (Hardback : alk. paper)
  1. Bridges—United States—Juvenile literature. 2. Royal Gorge Bridge (Colorado) [1. Royal Gorge Bridge (Colorado) 2. Bridges—Design and construction.] I. Title. II. Series.

  TG148.S64 2003
  624.2'3'0978853—dc22
                                                    2003015300

Table of Contents

An Engineering Masterpiece

SHEER CLIFFS OF pink, brown, and gray rock tower above the Arkansas River at the Royal Gorge in Colorado. From the middle of the Royal Gorge Bridge, the river appears to be a tiny trickle more than 1,000 feet below. When the spring thaw melts snow from the Rocky Mountains, however, the volume of water flowing through the gorge can increase from 250 cubic feet per second to 5,000 cubic feet per second. In a flash flood, the flow can increase to 10,000 cubic feet per second.

The Royal Gorge Bridge connects the north and south rims of the gorge. At 1,053 feet, the bridge is the highest suspension bridge in the world. The Royal Gorge is also home to the world's steepest incline railway and the site of the world's longest single-span aerial tram.

The bridge itself stands as a monument to the vision of a small group of businesspeople, politicians, and

Opposite:
The Arkansas River flows more than one thousand feet below the rim of the Royal Gorge.

The Royal Gorge Bridge opened in December 1929, after only six months of construction.

builders, who wanted the public to be able to enjoy the spectacular scenery of the gorge. Plans were suggested as early as 1905 to build a bridge over the gorge, but the land, given by the federal government to Cañon City, Colorado, in 1907 as a city park, languished for two decades without a clear vision for its use.

Finally, in 1929, vision and financial acumen combined in one visitor to the gorge. He was Lon Piper, a wealthy entrepreneur and bridge builder from Texas. Piper offered to provide the capital and supervise the construction of a bridge in return for operating leases that would allow him to collect tolls from traffic on the span.

Two months after Piper's proposal was approved by the Cañon City Council, construction of the bridge began. Six months later, in December 1929, the bridge opened to fanfare, speeches, a wedding in the middle of the roadway, brass bands, and a parade. Although the estimated building cost was $250,000, the bridge actually cost $350,000 to build. Despite the difficulties of working at one thousand feet above the river, no lives were lost during the construction of the bridge. The technical accomplishment of building the world's highest suspension bridge, combined with the excellent safety record, makes the Royal Gorge Bridge one of America's engineering masterpieces.

Types of Bridges

The Romans built hundreds of arch bridges and aqueducts; many, like this one near Nimes, France, are still standing.

There are three basic types of bridges: beam, arch, and suspension.

A beam is a squared-off log or a large, oblong piece of timber, metal, or stone used as a horizontal support in construction. A simple beam bridge is flat across and supported at the two ends. A log crossing a spring is an example of a simple beam bridge.

An arch is a structure, usually made of masonry, that forms the curved, pointed, or flat upper edge of an open space and supports the weight above it, as in a bridge or doorway. A simple arch bridge reaches across the river in an arching shape with a flat roadway on top, rather than straight across the river like the beam bridge does. An example of an arch bridge is the Pont du Gard, near Nimes, France. It was built shortly before the Christian era to allow the aqueduct of Nimes to cross the Gard River. The Roman architects and hydraulic engineers who designed this bridge, which features three levels of arches, created a technical as well as an artistic masterpiece.

A suspension bridge is a bridge that has the roadway suspended from cables that are anchored at either end and usually supported at intervals by towers. Some examples of suspension bridges are the Brooklyn Bridge, the Golden Gate Bridge, and the Royal Gorge Bridge.

Chapter 1

The Royal Gorge

THE ROYAL GORGE is noted throughout the world for its scenic beauty. That beauty, long known to Native Americans of the Ute tribe, went undiscovered by explorers of European descent until the early 1800s.

In 1803, Thomas Jefferson, the third president of the United States, signed a treaty to buy a huge tract of land from France. Known as the Louisiana Purchase, the land doubled the geographic area of the United States. At the time of the treaty, the boundaries of the Louisiana Purchase were vague, given as the entire watershed of the Mississippi River, including all tributaries.

In 1805, Meriwether Lewis and William Clark set off to explore the northern parts of the territory added to the United States by the Louisiana Purchase while a second group, led by U.S. Army lieutenant Zebulon Pike, explored the southern sections. One of Pike's

Opposite:
The Royal Gorge Bridge is the world's highest suspension bridge.

After the Louisiana Purchase treaty was signed (above), explorers set out into the new territory, which included the Royal Gorge.

missions was to locate the headwaters of the Arkansas River. The Arkansas, as the southernmost tributary of the Mississippi, formed one of the boundaries of the territory purchased by Jefferson. No one had ever mapped the region, and the source of the river was unknown. Pike arrived at the Royal Gorge on December 7, 1806. He wrote: "The river was merely a brook, bounded on both sides with perpendicular rocks, impracticable for horses ever to pass them."[1]

Pike's explorations and the westward expansion fueled by the 1848 discovery of gold near Sutter's Mill in what is now California brought settlers to the area near the gorge. Miners sought coal, iron, and other mineral deposits in the rugged mountains of Colorado's Front Range. By 1860, enough settlers had arrived to found Cañon City, the town nearest to the Royal Gorge. Cañon City residents flocked to the gorge, where they enjoyed picnic lunches and admired the view from the rim. They could look downward eleven hundred feet or walk along the top of the canyon walls. The sheer canyon walls made hiking into the gorge impossible, however. There was no route from top to bottom or from rim to rim.

Towns like Cañon City, Colorado (pictured), grew quickly during the westward expansion of the mid-1800s.

Explorers and settlers in the 1800s referred to the gorge as the Grand Cañon of the Arkansas. The name Royal Gorge was coined in the summer of 1874. According to an account in the local newspaper, the *Cañon City Daily Record*, a photographer named Mr. Savage, upon seeing the gorge, exclaimed, "This ought to be called the Royal Gorge!"[2]

Land for a City Park

By 1880, the Denver and Rio Grande Railway had constructed a railroad through the gorge. Visitors could enjoy the scenery as they traveled through the gorge in open observation cars on a railway that ran a few feet from the riverbed. Travelers were still limited, though, to looking up from the bottom of the gorge. One day, a local rancher named T.C. Johnson suggested that a bridge should be built across the gorge. He said, "If a Brooklyn Bridge could be built across that canyon, it would be the highest bridge in the world!"[3]

Visitors to the gorge included not only local residents, but travelers from across the United States. One frequent visitor to the gorge in the early 1900s was President Theodore Roosevelt. Roosevelt provided key support for preserving America's scenic beauty through the creation of parks and nature preserves. Other prominent leaders interested in promoting travel to the gorge included the governor of Colorado, James Peabody; Congressman Franklin E. Brooks; and the editor of the *Cañon City Daily Record*, Guy U. Hardy. The efforts of the men to create a park were success-

ful. On June 11, 1906, Roosevelt signed a bill that ceded five thousand acres of land to Cañon City "solely for park purposes and for the use and benefit of the public."[4]

President Theodore Roosevelt (center, in top hat) supported preserving America's natural places and often visited the Royal Gorge.

Twenty Years of Plans and Projects

With the land for the city park in hand, residents and businesses in Cañon City expected a boom in tourism. Early in 1907, a group of investors organized the

Cañon City and Royal Gorge Railroad Company. They intended to build a twenty-two-mile electric railroad to carry passengers from Cañon City to the rim of the Royal Gorge and to haul freight. The company raised $150,000, then began to grade the railroad bed, lay ties, and erect telegraph poles. The project cost far more than the investors had realized, however, and the company went bankrupt before the rails could be spiked down. In 1912, a second company tried to build an electric railroad and bridge. Their efforts, in turn, failed as a result of inadequate funding.

Despite the unfinished projects, the idea of building a bridge persisted. In 1925, Lorin Forgy, the owner of the gift shop on the north rim of the gorge, was granted an operating lease for the park and permission to build a footbridge across the gorge. His plans lacked financing, however, and investors proved unwilling to commit money to a project that had faltered twelve years earlier. Although the town council of Cañon City funded and built a road to the gorge, no progress could be made on the footbridge without outside capital. Forgy continued to operate the concession stands and shops at the gorge, but there was still no way to cross the chasm from rim to rim.

Lon Piper, Bridge Builder

In 1929, a builder named Lon Piper visited Cañon City and presented a new proposal. This one called for an automobile bridge across the gorge. Piper had two advantages over others who had tried to build a bridge: He knew how to raise construction funds, and he knew how to build bridges. He had already financed and directed the construction of three bridges over the Rio Grande between Texas and Mexico. In return for financing construction, his company was allowed to operate the bridges and receive revenue from the tolls people paid to cross them. Piper proposed the same kind of financial arrangement for the Royal Gorge Bridge.

The city council awarded Piper the contract to build the bridge on April 15, 1929. The next day, the *Cañon City Daily Record* reported: "The signing of the contract with Mr. Piper Monday night means that one of the greatest and most spectacular suspension bridges in the world is to be built across the Royal Gorge without delay. . . . The bridge will not only be the highest in North America, but one of the longest of the suspension type."[5]

Obstacles to the construction of the bridge surfaced immediately. There was no electric power at the site, and there was an existing contract between Cañon City and Lorin Forgy to build a footbridge. One of Piper's

15

Lon Piper agreed to finance the bridge construction; in exchange, his company received the tolls people paid to cross the bridge. This 1929 photograph shows a toll gate at the bridge.

first acts was to secure an agreement from Forgy that would grant Forgy's building rights to the newly formed Royal Gorge Bridge and Amusement Company. In return, Forgy would retain his shops, which had expanded to include a restaurant and observation pavilion, at the rim of the gorge.

As soon as the surveying began to determine a route for the power lines to be run, another potential obstacle arose. In Congress, Senator Charles Waterman of Colorado introduced a bill that would create a national park at the Royal Gorge. If passed, the bill would repeal the act of Congress that gave the land to Cañon City, and control of the land would revert to federal jurisdiction. The bill failed, however, and Piper began work on the bridge.

Workers' Lives

The majority of workers in the 1920s came from rural, agricultural backgrounds. Their education seldom included high school. Many children left school in their early teens to work on their family's farm.

The surveyor for the Royal Gorge Bridge was a man named Otis Witcher. Because higher education was far away and very expensive for people from rural communities, Witcher had obtained his training the way that many people did in the 1920s. He had taken correspondence courses and received his certification as a surveyor from the International Correspondence Course, a respected source for long-distance learning. Witcher's son Harold recalled that his father, because of his advanced studies, was considered to be a very highly educated man.

Other bridge workers came directly from farms and were trained on the job. The high wages, thirty to sixty cents per hour, plus the training in construction work made the job extremely attractive. In 1929, a loaf of bread cost eight to nine cents. A steak dinner in a restaurant cost seventy-five cents. Wages of sixty cents

Many of the people who worked on the bridge lived at the gorge during the construction, but their families lived in Cañon City (pictured).

per hour were considered to be very high pay. A worker could buy three meals per day, cooked and served to him in the company cook shack, for about one dollar. Work continued seven days a week, and crews stayed on the job ten hours a day.

Many of the bridge workers had family members who lived in nearby Cañon City. Wives, children, and parents of the workers visited the site and viewed the progress of the construction.

Chapter 2

The Bridge Begins

BUILDING ANY BRIDGE requires two major phases: design and construction. For the Royal Gorge Bridge, the design had to encompass specific geological features of the site. Construction would depend on moving building material and men to the gorge. Both phases of the building required skilled decisions by Lon Piper when he hired key personnel and acquired steel and other materials for the bridge.

Piper's first task was to hire the bridge engineer, who would design the bridge and oversee the construction. Piper chose George Cole, an experienced designer and engineer who had worked with Piper on his three bridges in Texas. Before these projects, Cole had designed and built a bridge over the Snake River in Washington State that, at the time of construction, was the highest bridge in the country.

Opposite:
The bridge designer, George Cole, faced many unique engineering challenges because the gorge was so deep.

Constructing a bridge over the Royal Gorge meant unique challenges. In the construction of a typical suspension bridge, there are two main elements: the towers and the suspension cables. The towers usually stand on piers that are built directly in the riverbed. The suspension cables are strung over the tops of the towers and anchored on both sides of the bridge. The roadway is then suspended from the cables. The cable anchorages are critical, for they are a major component that ensures the safety of the bridge. Without a solid system for anchoring the cables to the rims of the gorge, the suspension cables that support the roadway might come loose. Similarly, without solid foundations for the towers, the entire bridge—cables, roadway, and towers—would be in danger of falling into the gorge.

At the Royal Gorge, it was impractical to consider building towers more than one hundred feet tall at the bottom of the gorge to support the cables. That meant that the towers would have to be built on the rim on either side of the gorge. Instead of piers, the towers would be constructed on special concrete and steel foundations called abutments. This unusual design meant that the other bridge element, the suspension cables, would have to be securely connected to extra-strong anchorages on each rim of the gorge. To achieve the necessary strength for the cable anchorages, Cole designed a system of trenches on each rim of the gorge. At the bottom of each trench, pipes would be drilled into the granite bedrock. Wires would be anchored to the pipes, strung over the tops of the towers, and then anchored to the pipes on the other side. These wires

Usually, the towers of a suspension bridge rest on piers set directly in the riverbed. This was impractical for the Royal Gorge Bridge because of the gorge's depth.

would be bundled together to form the suspension cables. After the cables were completed, the anchoring trenches would be filled in with concrete.

The two cables that would hang from the towers and support the bridge would each be a quarter of a mile in length. It was critical that they be strong enough to carry the weight of the roadway and the

Each of the two cables that support the bridge is a quarter of a mile long and nine inches in diameter, and weighs about 150 tons.

vehicles that would travel on it. Cole originally intended to use eighteen hundred strands of galvanized number-nine wire to construct each cable. His design was reviewed by a colleague, railroad engineer O.K. Peck, who decided to increase the number of strands to twenty-one hundred.

With the contract awarded to Piper, and with the bridge design completed, the way was clear for the

greatest challenge of all—the actual construction of the bridge.

Construction Begins

Lon Piper's company, the Royal Gorge Bridge and Amusement Company, needed both workers and materials such as steel, fuel, machinery, lime, cement, lumber, and tools. Before construction could begin on  the bridge, all of the materials and workers had to be transported to the building site on the rim of the gorge. Most of the workers planned to live at the gorge during construction, as few of them owned cars or had the means to get back and forth from Cañon City to the site.

The First Steps: Roads and Electric Power

By June 4, 1929, Lon Piper had assembled enough workers to break ground for the bridge, but his supplies and workers could only reach one rim of the gorge. The old road, built in 1925, led only to the north rim. A road to the south rim had to be built to accommodate the flow of building materials. Along with the road, power lines were built to both rims of the gorge. Lon Piper promised that the bridge "will be brilliantly lighted at night, and half a dozen or more searchlights will be used for illuminating the depths of the Gorge."[6]

On June 10, workers began to build the road to the south rim. The route ran through hills that were solid granite, and the six-mile road took three weeks to complete. When the road was finished, large amounts of building materials began to arrive at the bridge site, along with more workers.

The Anchoring Trenches

The bridge's location required George Cole to create a design that integrated the two elements of suspension bridges, the towers and the cables, into the unique features of the Royal Gorge's landscape. The massive cables, which would weigh about 150 tons each when they were completed, would be anchored solidly into the rims of the gorge. The towers, also located on each rim of the gorge, would be set into foundations of concrete reinforced with steel. Cole designed both elements of the bridge to be strong enough to support the weight of the roadway, vehicles, and travelers.

As the road to the south rim was being built, workers used dynamite to blast trenches twenty-five feet deep and four feet wide into the solid granite bedrock of both rims. When completed, the anchoring trenches ran seventy-five feet in length.

Workers climbed into and out of the trenches using a series of ladders and hand-and-foot holds. Into the floor of each trench, men drilled two lines of holes that were nineteen inches apart. The holes went three feet deep into the solid rock. When the holes were completed, the workers drove a steel pipe, two inches thick, into each hole. There were one hundred of

these steel pipes in each trench. After each pipe was driven into place, the workers used grout to hold it in the hole and reduce any vibrations that might begin to work the pipe loose. The steel pipes would be used to anchor the wires for the suspension cables.

The towers were set into steel-reinforced concrete foundations on each rim of the gorge.

Chapter 3

Towers and Cables

As WORKERS INSIDE the trenches fitted steel pipes into the holes, other workers prepared the site for the concrete abutments that would be the foundations of the towers. Workers set steel beams upright inside deep holes blasted into the rock. Around the perimeter where the abutments would stand, the workers created wooden frames that defined the shape of the abutments. The amount of weight that would rest on the tower foundations was immense, including the weight of the cables, the towers themselves, the roadway, and, eventually, the weight of passengers and vehicles.

Crushed rock, which had been blasted out of the trenches, was mixed to make concrete. The workers poured the concrete inside the wooden frames and around the steel uprights. When the concrete dried and set, the workers built two derricks, one on each

Opposite:
Workers used derricks to lift the steel beams into place on the 150-foot towers.

27

rim. The workers used the derricks to lift the steel beams for the towers into place.

As the towers grew higher and higher, the workers had to climb up long ladders to reach the position where they would work for their shift. Working at different heights about the stony rim of the gorge, men drove rivets into the steel to secure the beams and crossbars. There was no safety net, and a fall meant a plunge onto the granite surface of the gorge's rim. Wind whipped through the gorge and caused the beams of the towers to sway. Workers clung to the beams as they hammered, pounded, riveted, and welded steel to create two 150-foot towers.

After workers bolted the last crossbars into place, they painted the towers. On September 13, 1929, the towers stood ready for the next step in the construction.

A High-Wire Act

With the towers in place, the bridge workers made preparations to string the first cables across the gorge. Like a high-wire act in a circus, construction work on the gorge took courage and a head for heights.

To string the first wires, two men, who each held a one-inch strand of wire, were lowered into the gorge. The men rode in steel tubs or buckets, which swayed in the wind as they made the one-thousand-foot trip to the floor of the gorge. When they reached the bottom, the men stretched the wires across the river and clamped them together.

Other workers at the top of the gorge pulled the clamped cable upwards. They reeled the wire out from

a gigantic spool so that the clamped section could be pulled to one side. An unbroken wire now reached across the gorge. Using hand winches, men stationed on the towers pulled the wire up and into the correct curve for the final suspension cables. All the other individual wires would be measured against this curve,

Although the men worked one thousand feet above the gorge, no serious injuries or deaths occurred during construction.

called the catenary, to ensure the proper sag for the suspension cables.

Inside the anchoring trenches, other men stretched the wire to the correct tension and clamped it into place. For the first time, there was a bridge from rim to rim across the Royal Gorge, even though it consisted only of a single one-inch-thick steel wire.

Stringing the Cables

To complete the suspension cables, each individual wire was strung across the gorge. The stringing process started when workers attached a guide cable to one end of a wire. Other workers operated power-driven carriers, machines like power winches. The carriers pulled the guide cable with the wire attached to it up one tower, across the span, and over the second tower. The wire was guided down from the second tower and clamped onto one of the steel pipes inside the anchoring trench. The guide cable would be attached to the end of a new wire and pulled back across the gorge.

A steel platform called the traveler hung from wires that had already been completed. Using the traveler, workers adjusted the tension of the new wire to ensure that it hung in the correct curve. After the workers reached the proper tension, the loose end of the wire was clamped onto a steel pipe. Every wire, all forty-two hundred of them (twenty-one hundred per cable), was individually strung across the gorge using this method.

Once twenty-one wires were clamped into place at the top of one of the pipes inside the anchoring

trenches, workers connected the wires to a reinforc-
ing bar, which was then grouted into place. The bars
extended to the top of the trench. The twenty-one
steel wires anchored to the one hundred pipes would
form the twenty-one hundred wires that made up

*Forty-two hundred
wires were indivi-
dually strung across
the gorge to complete
the suspension cables.*

each of the suspension cables of the bridge. The *Cañon City Daily Record* reported, "If placed in a single strand, [the wires] would reach from Cañon City to the Atlantic seaboard of New York."[7]

During the stringing process, workers stationed on the span itself made sure that the guide cable stayed in place as it was pulled up to the tops of the towers and across the gorge. After ten wires had been strung, workers bundled them together and secured them with steel collars. With the wires bundled together, the friction between the wires and the distance that the wires could swing in the wind were minimized. This part of the work was difficult and dangerous, as there was no roadway in place beneath the workers. If a worker looked down, he had an unobstructed view one thousand feet straight down into the riverbed. The men worked in high-altitude mountain conditions and in weather that could be windy, wet, and dangerous. Charles Driesel, a worker on the bridge, remembered: "The men wore overalls and shoes that had suction cups on the soles. . . . No one ever walked on the lumber and steel skeleton (of the bridge). You shuffled everywhere you went. Your feet never lifted."[8]

Lon Piper visited the bridge frequently. The project progressed without any serious injuries, largely due to Piper's leadership and his concern for the welfare of the workers. Piper believed in what he called "square dealing," both in his business ventures and in his commitment to his workers. This belief led him to cancel work on stormy days and to encourage safe practices on the bridge work site.

The Geology of the Royal Gorge

The Royal Gorge's scenic beauty results from two main forces: tectonics and erosion. Tectonics is the theory of how the earth's surface moves and folds. Erosion occurs when soil and rock are worn away.

The earth's surface, according to tectonics, consists of rigid plates that fit together like a huge, moving mosaic made of sixty-mile-thick tiles. Mountain ranges arise where one plate slips under another or when a plate folds upward in the middle. The rims of the Royal Gorge were formed out of an ancient seabed lifted up by this folding process.

The second force that helped form the Royal Gorge was erosion. During erosion, wind and water loosen and dissolve surface rocks or soil and carry them away from their original position.

Over millions of years, water from the Arkansas River gradually eroded the rocks that form the steep walls of the gorge.

Water that trickled down through cracks in the granite mountains wore through one thousand feet of rock to form the chasm of the Royal Gorge.

The World's Tallest Bridge

WHEN THE LAST of the forty-two hundred wires was attached and collared together with the other wires, the cables had reached nine inches in diameter. The workers then prepared the final step in the anchoring system. They poured concrete into the trenches to immobilize the ends of the wires. The bridge was ready for the finishing touches—the roadway, which would carry pedestrians and vehicles, and the wind system, which would control the amount of sway in the bridge to a safe level.

Workers hung one-and-one-eighth-inch steel suspender rods every ten feet along the suspension cables. Then they fitted fifteen-inch-wide-by-eighteen-foot-long floor beams horizontally into the bottoms of the suspender rods. The floor beams were attached from one cable's suspender rod to the other cable's corresponding suspender rod so that they formed a U, with

Opposite:
More than a thousand tons of structural steel and a thousand miles of steel wire were used in construction of the bridge.

When the bridge was finished, people were able to drive or walk across it to enjoy the spectacular scenery of the gorge.

the floor beams as the eighteen-foot-wide bottom of the U and the suspender rods as the sides of the U.

The floor beams in turn supported two lines of eight-inch I beams (beams with short flanges that are shaped like the letter I) and seven lines of eight-inch channel stringers (horizontal supports for the roadway). Lastly, the workers fitted three-inch planks on top of the I beams to form the roadway. The completed roadway was eighteen feet wide and a quarter of a mile long. The wood, like the steel and other materials, came from Colorado.

With the roadway completed, the last step in the construction could begin. The bridge needed to be protected from the wind that gusted through the Royal Gorge. If the bridge swayed too much, the cables, the support rods, and the flooring could wear against each other and possibly break from the increased friction. To keep the bridge level under most conditions, George Cole designed a unique wind system. Workers ran one-and-a-half-inch-thick wind cables to the canyon walls, where they anchored the cables into granite. They used guy wires to tie the bridge floor to the cables. Some of the cables ran more than one hundred feet below the floor of the bridge. The bridge still swayed up to nine feet in each direction. Even today, gusty storm winds can cause the bridge to close for safety reasons.

The final touches had been made. The bridge was ready for pedestrians and vehicles. In the six months of construction, no serious injuries had occurred. Workers, bridge engineer George Cole, financier Lon Piper, and everyone who had helped were all ready for the bridge's opening day.

A Celebration of the Opening

On December 8, 1929, the Royal Gorge Bridge opened to the public. Lon Piper and the bridge workers had accomplished their dream. On the morning of opening day, the world's highest suspension bridge stood waiting for the first pedestrians and vehicles to cross.

State, county, and city officials from across Colorado participated in the opening ceremonies at the Royal Gorge Bridge. The governor sent his greetings but was unable to attend due to poor health. At 3:00 P.M., the so-called Queen of the Celebration, a local girl named Opal Joyce, cut the ribbon to mark the official opening of the bridge. A marching band played "America" as it crossed the bridge. Joyce and the official party followed. On the south side of the bridge, the mayor of Cañon City, T. Lee Witcher, presented the bridge to the public on behalf of the Royal Gorge Bridge and Amusement Company.

According to the local paper, a throng of approximately ten thousand pedestrians attended the ceremony. A couple from Florence, Colorado, decided to hold their wedding on the bridge. Local members of the Lions and Rotary Clubs helped direct traffic. At the end of the day, Lon Piper gave a banquet for more than one hundred locals and out-of-town guests.

Opening day was celebrated with speeches, a parade, and even a wedding in the middle of the bridge.

More Ways to View the Gorge

With the opening of the bridge, a stunning accomplishment had been achieved. The Royal Gorge could be

The world's steepest incline railroad was built the year after the bridge was completed to take visitors to the bottom of the gorge.

crossed from rim to rim. Lon Piper's vision, however, extended beyond the bridge. He wanted to create a way for travelers to ride down from the rim to the bottom of the gorge. Construction of the incline railroad began soon after the bridge opened to the public.

Many men who had worked on the bridge stayed to build the incline railroad. The steep walls of the canyon and the difficult working conditions in the winter of 1929 to 1930 caused delays during the construction. The railroad construction took eight months, two months longer than the bridge. When the incline railroad was completed, passengers could ride to the bottom of the gorge, look up at the sheer granite walls, and observe the underside of the bridge. The incline railroad, a cable car system in which the weight of the ascending car counterbalanced the weight of the descending car, remains the steepest railway of its type in the world.

By the 1960s, thousands of visitors had crossed the bridge and ridden the incline railroad. The bridge operators began the construction of a new attraction, an aerial tramway. The tramway, similar to a ski gondola, opened on June 14, 1969. It carried passengers across the gorge in cabins that held thirty-five people. At the south end of the tram, trails along the rim allowed visitors to hike beside the gorge.

Reconstruction

Safety was a concern during the building of the bridge, and it has remained a priority throughout the bridge's lifetime. The bridge, the incline railroad, and the aerial tramway are given regular safety inspections. In 1984, an inspecting engineer discovered evidence of corrosion in the anchoring system. The trenches were completely excavated, and a completely reengineered system replaced them. Workers drilled fifty-five feet into solid granite as part of the new anchoring system. Once the new anchors were completed, workers replaced the wires one by one. The original construction of the bridge in 1929 cost $350,000. The renovation cost more than $3 million.

The Future of the Bridge

The bridge's operators continue to share the vision that led Lon Piper to create the Royal Gorge Bridge and Amusement Company in 1929. A living history center opened in 2002. Future improvements to the site include the creation of a wildlife sanctuary, programs on birds, student tours, and an educational center devoted to Colorado's natural history.

The world's longest single-span aerial tram was added in the 1960s to carry visitors across the panoramic gorge.

The Royal Gorge Bridge is considered to be an engineering and technical landmark. More than one thousand tons of structural steel and more than one thousand miles of steel wire for the suspension cables went into the construction of the bridge. All of the steel and wire was milled in Colorado. In six months, without any serious injuries, the bridge went from a dream to reality. The world's highest bridge remains a masterpiece of design, safety, and inventive engineering.

Thousands of visitors continue to visit the Royal Gorge and all of its attractions each year.

Notes

Chapter One: The Royal Gorge

1. Zebulon Montgomery Pike, *The Journals of Zebulon Montgomery Pike, with Letters and Related Documents.* Vol. 1. Norman, OK: University of Oklahoma Press, 1966, p. 335.
2. Quoted in "How The Royal Gorge Got Its Name," *Cañon City Daily Record*, May 11, 1911, p. 4.
3. Quoted in "World's Highest Bridge Conceived by Camp Man," *Cañon City Daily Record*, n.d.
4. Quoted in Bartell Nyberg, "Cañon City's Money-Making Gulch," *Denver Post*, August 9, 1970.
5. Quoted in "City Council Grants Right to Lon Piper," *Cañon City Daily Record*, April 16, 1929, p. 4.

Chapter Two: The Bridge Begins

6. Quoted in "Survey Made for Installing Power," *Cañon City Daily Record*, April 17, 1929, p. 3.

Chapter Three: Towers and Cables

7. *Cañon City Daily Record*," Gorge Bridge Towers Near Final Height," August 20, 1929, p. 6.
8. Quoted in John Salas, "Puebloan Recollects His Part in Royal Gorge High Wire Act," *Pueblo Chieftain and Pueblo Star-Journal*, May 10, 1980, p. 10.

Chronology

1806   First written record of the Royal Gorge by Zebulon Pike.

1874   Name changed from Grand Cañon of the Arkansas River to the Royal Gorge.

1907   Park land granted to Cañon City by the federal government.

1925   Road built to the top of the gorge.

1929   Lon Piper awarded the contract to build the bridge; bridge opens on December 8.

1930   Incline railroad built.

1960   Aerial tramway built.

1984   Bridge reconstructed after corrosion raises safety concerns.

2002   Living history center opened.

Glossary

catenary—The curve formed by a perfectly flexible, uniformly dense, and inextensible cable suspended from its endpoints.

galvanize—To coat iron or steel with rust-resistant zinc.

number-nine wire—Steel wire that is 0.1483 inches in diameter.

pier—A supporting structure at the junction of connecting spans of a bridge.

span—The extent or measure of space between two points or extremities, as of a bridge or roof; the breadth.

For More Information

Books

Joe Chapman and Dinah Jo Chapman, *Royal Gorge Bridge: A History in Words and Pictures of the Royal Gorge Region*. Canyon City, CO: Royal Gorge, 1965.

Halka Chronic, *Roadside Geology of Colorado*. Missoula, MT: Mountain Press, 1980.

Zebulon Montgomery Pike, *The Journals of Zebulon Montgomery Pike, with Letters and Related Documents*. Vol. 1. Norman, OK: University of Oklahoma Press, 1966.

Websites

Cañon City Chamber of Commerce (www.canon citychamber.com). This site includes photos and information on the history, arts, and culture of the region.

International Database and Gallery of Structures (www.structurae.net). This site includes details about bridges, photos, and a bibliography.

Royal Gorge Bridge and Park (www.royalgorge bridge.com). This site includes maps and photos of the park and links to other local websites.

Index